Financial
Self-Defense
for Investors

Financial
Self-Defense
for Investors

George Gutowski

INSOMNIAC PRESS

Library and Archives Canada Cataloguing in Publication

Gutowski, George, 1953-
Financial self-defense for investors / George Gutowski.

Includes bibliographical references and index.
ISBN 1-894663-94-2

1. Corporate reports. 2. Investments. 3. Finance, Personal. I.
Title.

HG4521.G88 2005   332.6   C2005-903405-X

The publisher gratefully acknowledges the support of the
Canada Council, the Ontario Arts Council and the Department of
Canadian Heritage through the Book Publishing Industry
Development Program.

Printed and bound in Canada

Insomniac Press
192 Spadina Avenue, Suite 403
Toronto, Ontario, Canada, M5T 2C2
www.insomniacpress.com

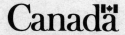

Internet Posting

On Sunday Feb. 10, 2002, at 2:26 p.m. ET, Msg 217564 on Yahoo's Enron Board, a poster leaves the message:

He that worketh deceit shall not dwell in my house; he that telleth lies shall not tarry in my sight. I will early destroy all the wicked of the land, that I may cut off all wicked doers from the city of the Lord.

Acknowledgements

I would sincerely like to thank all those whose help and encouragement aided me in producing this work. In particular, I would like to thank Daniel Varrette for his expert editing and advice on structuring. Also, I would like to thank Robert Mison and Peter Legein, both experienced businessmen who patiently read the book and provided valuable insight. Everyone's time is greatly appreciated. If there are any faults with the book, the responsibility resides with me.

Trick List

Preface

for
Market Manipulators, Swindlers,
the Ethically Challenged, and Those of the
Financially Twisted Persuasions

You need not read this book. You probably already know some or all of this stuff, especially the dirty parts. After all, you have been operating in the shadows and recesses tricking investors big and small. Some of you are petty; some of you have played a large game; some of you are probably incredibly good at this stuff.

Now some investors are going to catch on and catch up. However, if you are so inclined (perhaps you think I missed something), you may reach me via e-mail at georgegutowskiebox@hotmail.com

The honest person and truth seeker is now invited to read this book.

Introduction

Just what is this book? *Financial Self-Defense* is a primer for investors who worry about their money. Both institutional and individual retail investors experience worry. Worry is the great convergence of investing.

Worry is that emotion situated somewhere between *fear* and *greed*. Investors who pass successfully through worry, will hopefully reach *fear* and *greed* in a more enlightened and aware fashion. Those of you who go to *fear* and *greed* and do not spend requisite time at worry will impoverish yourselves. (Case studies pending.)

If you can learn to properly cycle through worry, your investments will perform better. Worry, quite frankly, is good. Think of the "wall of worry" as similar to the walls on military obstacle courses. First you doubt you can make it, then you try, then you learn, then you become disciplined, and finally you respect yourself as you have reached a higher level of discipline. Go to the higher level. It's more profitable.

The investment world has a great saying: *caveat emptor*—Latin for "buyer beware." A nice start for your money. So let's play the game. What do we *caveat emptor* against? How do we identify the sucker factor? How do we identify the potential of the sucker factor?

As investors approach the "wall of worry," they need to be mindful of who is encouraging them to go over. All those people shouting encouraging remarks are definitely not on your side. Investors can and should study both fundamental and technical analysis. What they often don't understand is the arcane craft of investor relations and how it is actually played and unfortunately misused.

How does investor relations affect the valuation process? Does it amount to anything, or is it just fluff? If companies did not perceive any value in it, they would not use it. [Hint to skeptic: most companies have an investor-relations function.]

What is investor relations? What are its objectives? What are the tools that are used and how do you recognize them? The judgment calls can and do go on forever. What is important is to understand how the professional and the not-so-professional play the game. Make no mistake: if you invest, you are in the game. The question is, how good are you?

This is not a book to slam the practice of investor relations (IR) and the IR community. There are many practitioners who are highly regarded. There are also many doctors, dentists, lawyers, accountants, and ministers who are well regarded. We do know that there are a number of professionals who need to hide under a rock. The higher the level of professionalism, the more easily they are able to bear scrutiny.

The individual needs to be able to critically evaluate IR activities. After all, they are using your money and should be responsible, preferably to you the investor.

The ethical IR practitioner need not be threatened. Many of you will be vindicated. Perhaps some of you will be cheering when you finish the book. Names are not being mentioned. I leave that for a later time. In the meantime, I am a fan of Eliot Spitzer. What we will focus on are the practices and the potential for abuse.

This book is designed as a series of short chapters with succinct take-away information. The reader can move from chapter to chapter as interests or needs dictate. The format is designed to make this information quickly understandable; there is enough obtuse financial information out there. My objective is to be simple and direct.

TAKE AWAY

**WORRY IS GOOD. LEARN TO EMBRACE IT.
FINANCIAL SELF-RESPECT COMES FROM DISCIPLINE.**

Chapter 1
Whose Interests?

What is investor relations (IR) and whose interests are being served? The National Investor Relations Institute (NIRI), a Washington, D.C.–based industry association, provides the following definition:

Investor relations is a strategic management responsibility using the disciplines of finance, communications, and marketing to manage the content and flow of company information to financial and other constituencies to maximize relative valuations.

One may conclude, therefore, that IR concerns itself with the development and execution of strategies designed to maximize shareholder wealth. Or does maximizing stock valuations concern itself with the development and execution of IR strategies? Which door do you want to enter? Do they sound the same? What are the real drivers? My current observation of investor relations concludes that it is management's attempt to occupy the investor's mind space in between trades.

Investor relations cannot guarantee a rising stock price or any stock price for that matter. But what investors should immediately note is that a critical component of IR is marketing. Yes, you are being marketed to—in fact, sold to. You are a customer; you are *the* customer.

Many analysts, brokers, and investors maintain that they cannot be influenced. They can see through the hype and make the correct moves. Behavioral psychology tells us there are beliefs and there are opinions. Using their beliefs and opinions, investors come to value judgments concerning stocks.

The process of arriving at a judgment can be shaped and influenced. The question becomes, how far upstream or downstream will you, the shrewd investor, allow those influences to enter into your thought process? In the final analysis, you need those influences before you can undertake one of four classic investment decisions:

Buy

Sell

Hold

Don't do it! (Ignore the stock. Potentially the most profitable investment decision available.)

A major objective of IR is to find and cultivate as many investors who will *buy* and then *hold* the stock on a long-term basis. Price is driven by supply and demand. If you take supply out of the market, you will help influence the price upwards. A conflict dynamic develops as IR attempts to put the best possible face on all circumstances and present compelling reasons to buy and hold. This may or may not be in the best interests of investors.

I am not aware of any IR program that presents reasons to *sell* or *ignore*. Some may feel this to be naïve. But whose interests are being represented and championed? Investors do not control the resources of the company. The investors must hone their abilities to read between the lines of regulator-correct, but investor-toxic materials.

TAKE AWAY

INVESTOR RELATIONS IS A CONVERGENT DISCIPLINE RELYING HEAVILY ON MARKETING.

INVESTOR-RELATIONS STAFFS WORK FOR MANAGEMENT, NOT INVESTORS.
THEY ARE NOT SPECIFICALLY APPOINTED TO REPRESENT THE SHAREHOLDERS AS AN AUDITOR OR SIMILAR INDEPENDENT PROFESSIONAL IS.

Chapter 2
Information Food Chain

Information is power, particularly in its timing. The timing of information shapes the exercise of power and determines the level of your empowerment or enslavement. As capital markets became more democratic and therefore competitive and egalitarian, information dissemination has continued to evolve in a positive fashion. The Internet has empowered investors not only to be informed but also to be able to act immediately. Regulation Fair Disclosure (Reg FD) has compelled companies to release all material information to everyone at the same time.

One of the major losers has been the brokerage community who used to rely on so-called insights (what is now considered to be insider information) to profit from price moves. Analysts were not all created equal and some were favored with preferred tidbits of information or insights that allowed them to gain advantage over other analysts.

Supposedly, this was passed onto the brokers who would call their clients, make exhortations designed as recommendations, and then move a lot of stock. Frequently, the price advantage was all but over and the retail investor was sheared.

With the advent of in-house traders—managing

ools of stock positions entirely independent and frequently in conflict with client investor positions—the analyst has many loyalties and disloyalties. Most employee analysts are legally beholden to their employer and therefore act accordingly. The concept of an independent analyst is problematic within the envelope of standard employment statutes.

It is not unknown for an analyst to attend an event with an activated cellphone dialed into the trading desk. The traders are waiting, with bated breath, for a buy or sell command. And guess what? When the analyst gets back to their desk, they may write up some research notes for distribution. Do you even get that stuff?

When Reg FD was being considered, the U.S. Securities and Exchange Commission (SEC) received a record amount of commentary, e-mails, letters, and other responses. Much of them were from the brokerage community who felt that it was not a good idea.

The investment dealer still carries a lot of clout for reasons I'll explain in later chapters. But given the nature of the business, the brokers and dealers still see themselves at the top of the food chain. They claim to be intermediaries, which means they touch the transaction before you do. Typically the touch is heavy-handed.

TAKE AWAY

TIMING IS CRITICAL.
THE PECKING ORDER IS STRATEGIC.

Chapter 3
Listen-Only Mode

With the advent of modern telecommunications, the analyst call was invented. Notionally, a telephone hookup was established, allowing management to talk to analysts. These were usually held following the quarterly results or whenever another major news item such as a takeover was announced.

The holy and accepted practice was to allow analysts only. Companies would brag about how they were highly selective as to who was invited and given the necessary passwords to get on. The proverbial A-List nonsense ran rampant. The financial media viewed this as a challenge and would routinely try to hack in. Of course, a reporter needed only to find a friendly analyst or portfolio manager, walk over to their office, and listen in on the speakerphone.

The listen-only mode terminology comes from the first part of the call when management speaks. Then analysts would queue up to ask questions. For large companies, this could mean hundreds. For small companies, quite frankly, no one was on and the company was "faking it until they made it."

The rationales for analysts were only as follows:

First, analysts did not want to be quoted in the financial media before they could formulate their thoughts and then issue their comments to their clients and customers. Most of the professional financial media does not quote analyst questions from conference calls. They will seek to interview the analyst separately if the event is newsworthy.

Second, it was widely held that the financial media was not savvy enough to understand the financial concepts and they would later be spoken to separately—basically a red flag in front of the bullfighting words. Many in the financial media can more than hold their own compared to analysts. They also do not have corporate finance or banking relationships with million-dollar fees affecting their judgment.

Most financial media outlets have strict codes of ethics regarding journalist and employee stock ownership. These codes may be more effective than the investment industry's attempts to regulate itself. Brokers sell stocks. Media sells headlines and news. What is the difference when they are both constituents of the chattering class?

Lastly, it was understood that retail investors would ask foolish questions and waste the time of professionals. There is no rational response for this supposition. Conventional wisdom also used to hold the world was flat, not round. We have been able to evolve over time on many different fronts and should continue to trust in the future.

Retail investors as a whole are on the intelligent side. They have investable capital and therefore have successfully passed through some of life's Darwinian selection trials. Perhaps the IR types do not recognize them as a legitimate constituency. If so, that is a danger signal of the sucker factor that may be embedded into the corporate culture and its governance.

As computer technology developed, companies became capable of webcasting their conference calls over the Internet. Now everyone with a computer and a decent Internet connection could participate. The call experience was also enhanced as PowerPoint slides could also be used to help communicate the message. This is particularly appealing given the volume of numerical and graphical information that everyone wants to rely on.

Guess what? This new technology is not being used to its fullest. The media and individual investors are allowed on, but in listen-only mode. However, there have now been changes in analyst behavior resulting from public scrutiny. First, it is still extremely rare (if not unheard of) for a buy-side analyst to publicly voice a question. Quite frankly, they do not want to tip their hands. If it became known that a particular fund was dissatisfied or very happy you would be able to predict its buy and sell activities. Therefore, you mostly only hear from sell-side analysts. When you do hear from a buy-side analyst, some will conclude they are promoting their holdings as they are finished buying.

Second, management gets to pick which analyst goes first and what the order will be (similar to the pecking order of the White House press corps). The management naturally picks favorites with the most management-friendly questions. Sell-side analysts are only too aware that their brokers have placed clients into stock and do not want to feel ambushed. Sell-side analysts also understand how corporate finance fees are earned and will not upset the apple cart.

Third, some analysts are still resisting the concept of doing analysis and focus on guidance. No one really springs any major surprises onto management. Occasionally, management has to promise to get back to the analyst on a particular question. Usually, it's in private.

Last, but not least, now that analysts realize the world is watching, they are using the opportunity to demonstrate how prescient they are by asking the supposedly clever question designed to rout out key information. Management is frequently bemused by how often they are seriously asked a question by an analyst whom they know already knows the answer. In fact, the question sounds good—sometimes very good—and all parties are well rehearsed. When the analyst sounds good, their stature goes up or stays up. Some investors actually listen to all this and do not realize how much theater and stage management goes on.

Management is always in control. The conference-call operator ensures that any one questioner can be connected at all times. Certain analysts who are known to be hostile never go live. In fact, the call may be concluded under the premise there are no further questions, when all the while a frustrated analyst has been gagged electronically.

The webcast technologies allow investors to submit questions by way of an online chat process. Companies who have tried this have found retail investors ask good questions. Investors of the retail variety are concerned with the issues as they affect their pocketbook and do not need to grandstand. Again, only management—not the listening public—sees the questions that are being submitted. I do not believe that enough companies are actually using this function.

The most important part of the call is the ability to

ask a question and critically evaluate and examine management. Unfortunately, some managements are pre-taping their remarks and then not taking questions. While this is a cheaper use of the various technologies, it is cynical in its application. The webcast is not live and may be edited to effect a slicker presentation. Managements that want to have the appearance of live presentations and then not accept any questions are suspect.

I have a final comment about webcasting and multimedia presentations. The investor needs to be aware of a fragmentation problem. Usually, the webcast has an associated press release. Frequently, PowerPoint presentations are used, especially for quarterly earnings calls. Just relying on the one item will not give investors the full perspective. Webcast technology allows for PowerPoint presentations to be integrated and fully synchronized so that an investor can correlate remarks to specific slides.

Many companies archive only the audio portion and provide the slides separately on their web sites. There are several aggregation services that provide links to various webcasts. If they do not also link into PowerPoint slides and press releases, investors may not be aware of their existence and will be at a disadvantage. If management created the materials believing that the exercise was useful, then all investors should evaluate the same material. Needless to say, the sucker factor could work against the investor.

Listen-only mode. Thank you, ladies and gentlemen, our next quarterly conference call is scheduled to be held on . . .

TAKE AWAY

INSTITUTIONS DO NOT WANT TO SHOW THEIR HANDS.
MANAGEMENTS CONTROL PROCESS AND FLOW.
QUESTIONS HAVE MORE SUBSTANCE THAN FORMAL PRESENTATIONS.

Chapter 4
Good Call Bounce

Buy on rumor, sell on news. Some stocks seem to run up before the earnings are announced and then sell off. Insider trading? Perhaps. When it becomes systemic—which I believe to be two quarters in a row—it is most likely attributable to short-term traders attempting to ride a cycle.

IR practitioners hate these traders because they have no loyalties to a stock beyond exceptionally short-term time frames, which may max out at the five-minute point. In fact, the short-term traders would be hard pressed to explain some of the finer points of the corporate fundamental story. The short-term trader selling off the stock in the face of good news becomes a target in the chess game. Management quite naturally wants this class of investor to be gone. Some strategies exist to ensure repentance. Most of the other investors do not appreciate the short-term, negative, technical effect of a sudden spike in stock volatility.

In some cases, IR management can soft manage expectations, guidance, and other intangible factors so that the analysts coming off the call will issue favorable comments and increase buying support. Traders selling will see the stock increasing in value and will stop or reverse their orders, causing the price to bounce upward.

The game of "cat and mouse" starts as traders attempt to discern if guidance will be changed either on or off the call. Guidance does not have to be spoken to when quarterly results are announced. The quarterly statements are all rear-view-mirror exercises. If the company is strong and has growing revenues, it can manufacture a "good call bounce." If enough traders get seriously burnt, they will start to respect the stock and hopefully leave it alone.

Management is somewhat stymied before the earnings announcement by something called a "quiet period" or blackout. This is the time frame from the end of the quarter to when the results are publicly announced. The accounting department is feverishly working up the statements. Management has an idea of how the results are coming together. They cannot buy or sell stock themselves or make any public comments about the earnings. Employees—as well as their 401Ks and other holdings—are usually subject to the same regulations.

The short-term traders take the opportunity to ride around the proverbial fort whooping and hollering knowing that they probably will not be shot back at. But they raise hell in the meantime. Then, the cavalry finally arrives with the earnings announcement. One of the better ways to curtail this short-term volatility is to accelerate the release of information and reduce the quiet-period time frame.

TAKE AWAY

QUIET PERIODS ADD TO UNCERTAINTY.
ANTICIPATION SOMETIMES EXCEEDS REALITY.

Chapter 5
Very Late-Breaking News

Securities law has long compelled companies to release material information. The question of tactics develops. It's only natural to want to emphasize good news and minimize bad news. So what are the tactics? First, let us try to understand how some aspects of the news cycle work.

Most news organizations will have some form of morning meeting where they attempt to plan out the day's efforts. At this point, there is maximum flexibility. Headlines have not yet been selected. Editors and electronic producers are still surveying the landscape looking for the big one—the lead story. As the day progresses, the inevitability of deadlines grows and decisions start to form. At first they are soft, and then with the passage of precious time, the decisions harden.

Clearly, what would attract attention early in the morning may be bumped by a better story and then relegated to page fourteen or even discarded if it comes out late in the afternoon. The lesson for bad news is obvious. If there is any way of sitting on the story until later in the day, do it. You have now increased the probability of attracting less attention. You have also met all your disclosure requirements and are completely clean from a regulatory perspective. [Hint to manipulators: hold the bad-news board meetings in the afternoon—late in the afternoon—if you catch my drift.]

There is also a school of opinion that summarizes traders: investors and brokers go into information overload as the day moves on. With the exception of cataclysmic news, they may be likely to miss or discount bad news. It's worth a shot.

The extension of this is to release information on Fridays or the day before statutory holidays; long weekends are best. The premier business news-shows stand down for the weekend and are not looking for news. Print periodicals, predominantly weekend newspapers, frequently change their focus from hard and late-breaking corporate business news to more perspective-laden offerings such as financial planning, economics, career planning, and the op-ed piece.

I remember being a new employee at a news wire several years ago. I did not have any seniority so I was stuck working Christmas Eve. I was shocked to see the activity level of new press releases coming in. There was a preponderance of tough or bad news that was slowly being bled out into the marketplace. Season's Greetings?

My suggestion to the crusading business journalist looking for a "scoop": look at the companies who are releasing late in the cycle, especially before weekends and holidays. If you notice a pattern, you could conclude: "Where there's smoke, there's fire."

TAKE AWAY

BE VERY AFRAID OF "FREAKY FRIDAY."

Chapter 6
Now You See It.
Now You Don't.

There are rigorous regulations on disclosure. Essentially, the intent is to release material information as soon as possible. For historical reasons, this flow of information has been outbound to the financial community. Web sites are still a relatively new tool. Regulators are only insisting that they be accurate. They also insist that information not be posted exclusively on a company web site. Roger, so far.

But how long should material stay up and how long does it stay up? The news media is not compelled or regulated. They trade on the currency of information. Dated material goes in archives of various descriptions. These archives typically may only be accessed for a fee. Depending on the costing structure, the individual investor may find this expensive and certainly inconvenient. Government web sites such as the Electronic Data Gathering Analysis and Retrieval (EDGAR) electronically maintain certain documents that regulators demand. Most of these documents are obtuse and the sites do not win awards for usability.

Corporate web sites do not have any regulatory framework defining how long materials must stay available. While most IR professionals will publicly argue for consistency, the reality is different. There is a lot of discretion used as to what material is kept up and how prominently it is positioned. Regulatory-mandated material such as 10-Ks (a type of detailed annual report) is available by link to SEC/EDGAR. The other materials, any of which are not SEC-format documents, are managed at the discretion of corporate management. One is reminded of the Billy Crystal citation, "It is better to look good than feel good."

Of particular concern is the access to quarterly conference calls. Many companies do not keep the calls up for longer than a week and many of them neglect to maintain an archive of all the calls. Culpable IR practitioners will argue that they do not want to confuse investors and provide access to multiple calls. Yet, it is common practice to maintain historical financial statements, which could be downloaded in portable document formats (PDF).

I have never been comfortable with the "do not confuse the investor" argument. My concerns revolve around the ability of new investors to have the same access to information that existing older investors have been able to use. Also, existing investors may wish to revisit material and may find it no longer available.

The practice of making material disappear provides the ability for abuse at its worst. In the best-case scenario, by changing the weighting of materials from prominent to secondary to non-existent, the investor is offered the opportunity to shape conclusions in a subtle, yet compelling fashion. Many messages creep.

Many in the IR community speak of the investment mosaic. This recognizes that the perceptions in the marketplace are the sum result of many variables such as annual and quarterly reports, press releases, conference calls, web sites, regulatory material, etc. While the company constructs the mosaic, the investor must understand that the passage of time is not equal for all the pieces. If it is negative, the corporate scissors will come out as soon as possible.

TAKE AWAY

INVESTMENT MOSAICS ARE DYNAMICALLY MANAGED; AND STORIES, POLISHED.

Chapter 7
Basking in the Limelight

Some companies are leaders that have coattails. Whenever they make an announcement, they automatically garner attention. Because of their market-leadership position, they possess a prestige value that associated partner companies seek to exploit.

The weaker companies will always make a big fuss that they are now dealing with, are continuing to deal with, and/or will continue to deal with a particular entity. While it is always good news when a positive relationship has developed or is being extended, investors should focus on why the relationship is attractive and who the marquee client is.

If a large client base of Fortune 500 clients is developing, then there is substance to the product offering. Initially, as the company is acquiring clients, its attempt to leap into the limelight should be taken with a pinch of salt. When reading the press release, the investor will notice how the company is gushing over the relationship, frequently quoting the marquee company's senior officers. The underlying transaction is often a loss leader or, at best, has razor-thin margins. The point of the exercise was to get the marquee name on the client list. The marquee name knows this and negotiates ruthlessly.

A common maneuver is to arrange for the press release to be issued jointly and rely on the drawing power of the marquee client to stimulate the market. Large marquee companies that are sensitive to the needs of smaller partners will issue corporate communications announcing various transactions. In many cases, the transaction is not material for the marquee client. There is a stamp of approval and authenticity that is being granted. The sucker factor develops when the dominant partner and/or employees are in a unique position to trade on information long before the market realizes what is happening. There are many different ways to leak this information. Some of these press releases may announce several unrelated transactions. Unfortunately, for the smaller company, they may be lost on a large list.

TAKE AWAY

DETERMINE WHOSE NEWS THIS REALLY IS.
COMPANIES MUST EVENTUALLY STAND ON THEIR OWN.

Chapter 8
E-mail Alerts

Have you ever received non-stop unsolicited e-mails? Have you ever opted into a list and then received lots of junk you never wanted? Have you ever signed up for e-mail alerts specifying which stocks and what kind of news you want? Gotcha! All these services are free to the recipient. (*Quelle surprise!*) Operating on the time-tested paradigm that there is no such thing as a free lunch, why use them?

As an investor, you need to monitor your investments. If you are not in a position to sit in front of a monitor with real-time data, you will need to be reachable. So e-mail alerts to your personal digital assistant (PDA) device, cellphone, or e-mail program become a valuable tool. Most companies will encourage you to register for e-mail versions of their press releases. (This is somewhat impractical as you will invite information overload if you follow many companies.)

Third-party services will feed you information relatively soon after it has been released. What is relatively soon? The concept of timely is not always expressed in mathematical terms. The alert service certainly has no regulatory responsibility as to the timeliness of its delivery. Let's take a step back and explore the revenue model for an e-mail alert service.

Initially, these services had hoped to profit from advertising. We now know that while some revenue is possible, Internet ads will not pay all the bills, much less lead you to profitability. The public companies themselves and other interested parties will pay for the e-mail service (frequently in combinations of stock and cash). The company can claim that it is attempting to widely disseminate information. I would buy into that story only if it uses that service for all its press releases and not just the good stuff.

The interested party can be anyone who clearly has an interest in the stock. Their interest may or may not be aligned with your interests. They are pursuing their interests with very little liability for even the strongest statement. Laws about lying are difficult to uphold. Many of these services actually market access to their lists just as direct-mail list brokers market their lists.

The difficulty comes in the need to make a dynamic real-time decision as to whether this is authentic news or whether this is a conclusion or opinion that has been massaged to influence your actions. In other words, the sucker factor applies in this situation.

The best way to trigger these e-mail alerts is through the use of stock symbols in a press release. Many of the alert programs monitor large news-wire and press-release services and automatically pick up a story that has a stock symbol and just resubmit it. All you have to do is issue a press release containing a stock symbol and perhaps your opinion on the company's prospects and out it goes.

IR practitioners frequently subscribe to monitoring services so that they can pick up who is talking about them. The idea will be to build bridges and develop a professional relationship. Sometimes they determine that the sources are hostile and/or toxic. In these cases, the sources will be flagged and the legal departments alerted. Stopping them is very difficult, if not impossible.

As a practical matter, investors have to recognize the environment they work in. Can you actually read and comprehend an e-mail alert at work? Or are you in an environment with constant meetings, travel, etc. that functionally either prohibits or makes it exceptionally difficult to read and respond? You could be a doctor or dentist who cannot turn away from your responsibilities or you could be a blue-collar worker on the assembly line. Many people are not able to immediately respond. This does not mean you give up on investing, but you have to realize that a strategy requiring you to be nimble on a moment's notice may have a self-induced sucker factor.

TAKE AWAY

UNDERSTAND WHERE THE MESSAGE IS COMING FROM AND WHY.

Chapter 9
Rolling Thunder

Any advertising executive or educator will confirm that repetition helps get the message out. But many entities are criticized for not communicating well. The criticism sometimes comes from those who are distracted and did not focus on the message when it first came out. Also, with information overload and competition for mind space, the one-shot golden bullet does not exist. Essentially, you either go nuclear with a devastating impact or you must make use of rolling thunder.

A few nation states and perhaps some evil terrorist groups can go nuclear to state their message. By default, for the rest of the world, rolling thunder becomes the tool of choice. How does it work? The message has to be delivered over and over again in a consistent fashion. You need to stay on topic and keep tapping on the wedge to drive home your point. Observe the difficulty of dealing with guidance and analyst forecasts. Despite the concept of consensus, there can be a fairly wide divergence in expectations on the street. Some of the divergence can be attributed to sloppy analysis and not getting the story correct. You would think that the Darwinian nature of investing would correct this problem.

However, if management is not communicating well, the street will develop inaccurate perceptions that will result in a surprise when earnings and other announcements are made. The street hates uncertainty and will punish the stock by driving it down. In reality, the street only hurts itself. Not everyone can sell at the same time so only a few can reduce their positions. The remaining investors who numerically must be in the majority are left with lower valuations and a chagrined view of management.

What does rolling thunder entail? Numerous press releases with different angles but leading to the same destination. Conference calls and webcasts discussing the specific issue will be rolled out. Innumerable media interviews by many senior officers within a very short period of time. When the financial media is savvy they will start to comment on the communications program as much as the supposed substance. Suddenly, it's pointed out that the PR machine has been cranked up. This will infuriate the IR professionals and perhaps confuse or irritate senior executives. Scrutiny will validate. If the thunder is viewed as too much campaign and not enough substance, the program should be panned. The company goes on the suspect list and next time, hopefully, there is a heightened sense of skepticism.

TAKE AWAY

WHILE COMMUNICATION IS RAPID, MESSAGES MAY HAVE A SLOW BURN.
WHILE MANAGEMENT IS CRITICIZED FOR COMMUNICATING POORLY, INVESTORS PAY WITH LOWER STOCK VALUATIONS.
IF YOU PAY ATTENTION PROPERLY, YOU CAN ACTUALLY GET AHEAD OF THE MARKET.

Chapter 10
The President Came in Today!

While there are many legitimate reasons to undertake a communications program, the investor needs to be aware of any bogus activity. Usually, a company will issue a flurry of press releases within a very short period of time. Each release will purport to cover material information, which should be disclosed. In fact, the news may be quite thin. The story may actually be fractured into several components to justify additional press releases.

The tactic attempts to create a sense of activity, hoping that investors notice and then decide to get on the bandwagon. The IR staff will rely on cleverly worded headlines hoping that the headline buzz sticks. When successful, the bandwagon starts up and momentum surges forward. If the IR staff is clever they will even pick (or luck into) slow news days when the media clamor is down a few decibels.

This move is akin to a duck furiously flapping its wings on the water to create some momentum. If you have ever observed a duck starting off, the initial effort is incredibly intense followed by an uneventful gliding swim that is unremarkable since it is calm. This is certainly a favorite technique of the pump-and-dump tactician. The cynical observer euphemistically refers to the press-release content as "the president came in today." This is not news; this is what is supposed to be happening. This tactic is a most blatant direct play into the sucker factor.

TAKE AWAY

READ THE PRESS RELEASE AND NOT JUST THE HEADLINE. READ ALL THE PRESS RELEASES, ESPECIALLY IF THERE ARE A LOT OF THEM IN A SHORT PERIOD OF TIME.

Chapter 11
Boiler Room Redux

Old-fashioned boiler rooms, for those who do not know, were usually located in cheap basement facilities—hence the financial term: boiler room. The promoter would then run in a series of telephone lines, hire a series of expert telephone salespeople, and start a massive outbound telemarketing campaign to known and suspected suckers, all of whom have a reasonable probability of actually sending in money to buy stocks.

At times, the stocks would not exist and some boiler rooms would not even be able to issue statements. This was outright theft and preyed on gullible investors. Eventually, they would disappear—usually one step ahead of the bunko squad—never to be heard from again. How the phone company agreed to install so many telephone lines in such an unlikely place is beyond my comprehension.

The more sophisticated scam was to act like a bona-fide broker dealer, maybe even be properly registered. While there were many variations to the scam, the investor essentially was induced to buy stock from the promoter's special inventory. Because of the intensity of "the promote," you had an artificial level of very high demand.

Investors were not allowed to sell. In many cases, investor sell orders were ignored. By inflating the stock, the price would naturally go up. This creates excitement and attracts more suckers. Frequently, the "tape was painted" with trades designed to make the stock go up. The general investing public would catch wind of the price movement and pile on, usually against the advice of ethical brokers, creating more upward pressure.

Can you guess the ending? The promoter would be selling stocks at exorbitant prices that were acquired at extremely cheap prices. When the supply was sold, "the promote" would be over and the bubble would collapse. This is illegal; and regulators as well as ethical industry participants have stamped out the old-fashioned version of theft.

Many, but not all, investors know better than to pay attention to the hard-charging, hard-sell promote from the old-fashioned boiler room. But can you spot the new boiler rooms? Do you even know when to get suspicious? *Boiler Room Redux* is certainly playing in the sucker zone near you. The end-game has not changed. The techniques are leading edge and evolving. Like most criminal activity, if the energy had been channeled into legitimate business, the business community would have lauded great accomplishments.

Many boiler-room-redux varieties are under the guise of investor relations/communications or investment newsletters. Since we are a free society, there is no requirement to register with a regulatory body or even join some form of self-regulating professional association. Needless to say, these practitioners do not engage in peer review. They do feel that they can rely on the First Amendment guarantee of free speech.

The newsletter scam starts with a historical review of the market. Using the 20/20 perspective of hindsight, the scammer picks the best gains as buy recommendations and the bigger losers as sell recommendations. They will then go through the sham of putting together a series of newsletters that look like they have been operating for quite some time. Needless to say, their track record is enviable. Very few credible professionals would be able to match it.

When you become aware of the newsletter, you are now promised the same, if not better, performance with the latest picks. The more sophisticated scams will include picks of popular and large-cap stocks. This looks good and hides their true intent. Laced throughout the process will be the select few that they really want you to buy.

The investor already knows about the relative investment merits of Cisco or Microsoft, thank you very much. The large-cap stocks may have been selected as a potential filter to pre-screen investors. After all, how many times have you heard the refrain "If only I had bought Microsoft or Intel back in the '80s?" But that stock trading at just $0.50 looks very intriguing. In fact, it looks a lot like Microsoft did in the early days. The newsletter will even shamelessly point this out. At the very least, the prestige of the large-cap "paints the target" in a positive limelight. The investor concludes either one of two things: I'll buy some now (after all, they reason, it's not a lot of money) or I'll wait and watch.

Next month, the new installment arrives electronically, as the modern thief understands the fundamental precepts of business (i.e. keep costs down). Besides, the subscriber gets the information much more quickly right there on the computer where they can just click away on their online account and put in a buy order.

In the intervening time, the stock has perhaps started to move up a little. It's certainly north of $0.50, but not in sell territory. The newsletter provides updates as to the positive aspects of the investments and just continues to prime the pump. The investors who bought are not discouraged and may in fact buy more. Of course, the stock is still deemed to be in the buy and accumulate zone. The investors who are watching from the sidelines are again encouraged to buy, as the train appears to be leaving the station.

Additional installments arrive announcing the same sort of activity. The newsletter may even start to show you how this is similar to other profitable opportunities where prices would increase dramatically. Well, you should know the rest of the story. Momentum builds. You buy. You buy more. You tell your friends. Your broker may notice and may get on the gravy train with other clients. Buzz builds and the stock climbs.

The newsletter promoter is selling into the rally. The stock value reaches a nosebleed level and finally the newsletter announces, if they are still around, that the stock is fully valued and should be considered as a long-term hold. They may pontificate about how this should be a core holding as it is attractive to other senior players who may be prepared to buy at a further premium.

So what's illegal about it? The newsletter must disclose if it is holding a position in the stock. The SEC routinely fines individuals who do not disclose they have a position. Small publicly traded companies will make deals with newsletter promoters to write up favorable reviews. They will pay in either cash or options that vest immediately and can or may be exercised at the discretion of the newsletter writer.

A variation of the scam is to accumulate shares without the knowledge of management and then pump the stock. The regulators may notice the price movement and naturally check with management to determine if news is pending. A befuddled management may quite legitimately be at a loss to explain the price movement. The regulator should at that time request that management issue a press release indicating that they are not aware of any material events that may affect the stock price or that could explain the recent run-up.

This is a heartbreaker as many investors will bail out and stay away. The unscrupulous newsletter operator will have substantially sold out the held position. The cynical operator may even be able to show that they have been buying the stock in good faith and have also experienced losses. We all know about offshore accounts and how you can hide from U.S. regulators.

A further variation of the scam is to build up a following and then approach management and blackmail them. Essentially, the threat is "I'll issue sell recommendations and paint a black picture unless you pay me to be a good boy." (Much like a protection racket run by the mob.) Unfortunately, the smaller companies are more susceptible to this. The only answer is to contact the SEC and the FBI and sting these types. However, this is difficult and on a good day can still make the company look confusing. Uncertainty kills your price. Consequently, a variety of moral dilemmas develop. Management may find itself dealing with the devil. My conclusion, as always, is the devil has never been a good business partner.

TAKE AWAY

CHECK OUT THE NEWSLETTERS. PUBLIC REPUTATION IS CRITICAL. SCOUNDRELS LIKE TO OPERATE IN THE SHADOWS AND CANNOT OR WILL NOT JEOPARDIZE THEMSELVES WITH PUBLIC SCRUTINY. NEWSLETTERS SHOULD DISCLOSE WHAT, IF ANY, FINANCIAL INTEREST OR CONNECTIONS THEY HAVE WITH THE MANAGEMENT OF A COMPANY. THERE IS NOTHING ILLEGAL ABOUT BEING PAID TO PROMOTE A STORY. WE SHOULD ALL KNOW WHAT LEVEL OF INDEPENDENCE THERE IS AND WHAT THE CONTEXT IS.

Chapter 12
Chinese Walls, Sell-Side Analysts

Some investors feel that analysts are supposed to be independent. This is a diminishing crowd and will soon be on the endangered-species list. Analysts are supposedly influenced or claim adherence to professional standards. There is even a designation, which is bloody tough to get. Called the chartered financial accountant (CFA), it mandates a three-year program followed by grueling exams at the one-, two-, and three-year marks. Most people fail, making the CFA a rigorous designation that deserves respect in the marketplace. So why do some analysts issue buy recommendations at high prices, watch the stock tumble into the basement, and then issue a sell? Excuse me, but isn't "buy low, sell high" part of the fundamental arithmetic that applies to investing? Buy high and sell low does not work. Skeptics, upon adequate research, should refer to their brokerage accounts.

For the uninitiated, there are two sides to the street. The buy side consists of the institutions and the individuals who actually own the stock and have put their precious capital at risk. The other side is referred to as the sell side. Essentially, they are the intermediaries who bring the companies to market and convince investors to buy the shares when originally underwritten. The two functions can be at odds. On the very best day, they have radically differing perspectives on the market. When one side is buying and the other side is selling, you observe opposing views. (Relying on the sellers' tout has proven to be one of the major sucker plays of the decade.)

Consequently, the terminology of buy-side and sell-side analysts has come into being. Buy-side analysts are not as vocal as the sell-side analysts are. If a buy-side analyst tips their hand and the market sees them coming, there can be disastrous results. The sell-side analyst has quite a different role: they are there to beat the drum and attract attention. They are frequently called cheerleaders, and if they are bad at it, they are turned over.

In its purest form, the sell-side analyst researches stocks and makes recommendations to the brokerage force. Investors supposedly rely on this information. When the research analyst was beholden to the stock brokers, there was pressure to stimulate demand and interest in the stock, which would drive trading volume through the firm's accounts, generate commissions, and everyone lives happily thereafter. While you should take everything with a grain of salt, the analyst and the heavily influential brokers realized that if they burned out their clientele, they would fail and revenues would dry up. (Not to mention the probable lawsuits.) There was a market discipline to get it right or you would be fired.

The investment business changed. Stock brokerage revenues experienced pressure with the rise of discount and online trading. Investment banking and corporate-finance activities started to generate huge fees. Corporations looking to raise capital would pay enormous fees. The competition for business intensified. The analyst became a tool of the investment-banking department. The investment banker was always looking for the next multi-million-dollar fees. At these prices, they would live for today and tomorrow be damned.

Analysts soon determined that they could not and would not bite the hand that feeds them. Analysts became cheerleaders extraordinaire and were more responsible for herding the market into the valuation the investment bankers wanted. The change was foisted on the market without many of the smaller investors recognizing the implications. When the market was rising, all boats floated rather well. Everything worked and living was easy.

The institutional side of the street had long been suspicious of the sell-side analyst. Recognizing that they needed and wanted their own independence, they essentially built their own infrastructure. The staff was either directly employed or independent analysts were contracted for their expertise. Several investment-dealer firms started on the premise that they do not do underwritings and therefore their research was not suspect. I concede: not as suspect. There was still a requirement to generate volumes and pay the bills.

TAKE AWAY

SELL-SIDE ANALYSTS WILL NOT BITE THE HAND THAT FEEDS THEM. YOU GET WHAT YOU PAY FOR. WHEN RESEARCH IS FREE OR CHEAP, BEWARE.

Chapter 13
The Lure of the Fee: Investment Banking

In days of old, new issues were underwritten on the basis of demand at an attractive price. This is probably one of the few businesses that have not really changed. When a company looks to issue new securities, the underwriter does not like being left with an inventory to carry. Just like a retailer, if you cannot sell product, it's dead capital. Inventory has to turn quickly or financial calamity ensues.

As long as everyone understands and can identify on sight the different species of flesh-eating sharks, then by all means please jump into the shark tank. In addition to some rather large fees paid to the investment bankers, not to mention accountants and lawyers, there are several aspects of the underwriting arrangement that the investor should recognize.

Frequently, the lead underwriter and some of the co-underwriters are obligated to establish and maintain analyst coverage. This can be a contractual obligation. The investment bank will say, of course, they follow the stock—after all, they underwrote it. Evidently, there is a lack of independence as various background factors can come into play.

The underwriter may require that certain blocks of shares be restricted, meaning the owners of these shares are not allowed to sell on the open market and cash out. This is designed to allow the market to trade and find its own levels. It helps signal that existing shareholders are not looking to dump their holdings.

The unfortunate consequence is that additional buying is manufactured as management, employees, and others seek unencumbered stock, forcing the stock upwards. Many of these investors already hold large positions and therefore their objectives are very short term and only increase volatility. When the restrictive periods expire, you can be sure that there will be selling. It's like watching an elastic band snap back.

TAKE AWAY

INVESTMENT BANKING IS A BUSINESS UNTO ITSELF. BUSINESSES ARE RESPONSIBLE TO THEIR SHAREHOLDERS. WHEN INITIAL PUBLIC OFFERING (IPO) ACTIVITY SURGES, OWNING SHARES OF INVESTMENT BANKS CAN BE A BETTER IDEA THAN THE IPO ITSELF.

Chapter 14
Annual General Meetings

The annual general meeting (AGM) is supposedly the signature event for a company and its shareholders. Based on democratic concepts, the shareholder has the right to question management, bitch and complain as appropriate, and vote for the board of directors. The annual meeting process is based on pre-technology suppositions. The reality is that most shareholders today do not attend the AGM. The meeting is physically inconvenient and uneventful in terms of information. Most individual shareholders consider their relative holdings to be small and therefore do not feel empowered to act as shareholders. And not to mention the impossibility of trying to attend five, ten, maybe more annual meetings while holding down a day job.

It's hard to argue with the above. Management takes advantage of the "do not attend" dynamic and naturally works it to their benefit. They handle most of the proxy-solicitation process. Directors are nominated by management and only voted on by shareholders.

With the advent of webcasting and secure e-commerce, it's possible for shareholders to attend electronically and vote on resolutions and directors. What unsettles management is the ability to vote from remote locations. Until now, the proxy-solicitation process was a time-forward process that allowed management to determine the voting results well in advance of the AGM.

AGMs may be levered to create a buzz factor. Usually, there are press releases that include statements from senior officers. Following elections of directors are more announcements. Very rarely has a routine AGM generated any surprise. The event is just used to beat the corporate drum and reinforce any existing messaging already underway.

TAKE AWAY

SHAREHOLDERS HAVE ABDICATED THEIR POWER AT ANNUAL GENERAL MEETINGS.
SHAREHOLDER ACTIVISM, WHILE IMPORTANT, IS DIFFERENT FROM INDIVIDUAL INVESTING. LITTLE PEOPLE CANNOT FIGHT BIG BATTLES.

Chapter 15
Story Pitch

A few words about how someone or something gets media coverage. The investor should understand that there is something called the story pitch. Basically, the IR functionary calls up a contact in the media and suggests or pitches an idea for a story.

The media is perpetually looking for new and interesting news items. Trade journals in particular are tasked with covering an industry segment and are quite interested in what is going on. The large mainstream circulations are more interested in the big story. There is a seam between the front page of the large circulations and the trades.

Essentially, page-two coverage is better than nothing. Many companies are only too happy to be covered. The publication may bank a few background-type stories for slow news days so as to flesh out their content and everyone is happy.

The writer who is always subject to deadline time pressures is more prepared to be influenced by the IR professional and usually appreciates all the background information and press kit materials that can be provided. The writer's objective is to create a piece that will help their career. Since the subject of the article does not usually have a big profile, the journalist is more inclined to want to tell a compelling story and bring something new into the world. Some journalists develop certain specialties or beats.

The trade journals should have more knowledge-able writers in their specialties. If, as an investor, you prefer to follow certain industry segments, subscribe to some of these publications and follow the buzz. Participants within a certain industry will quite natu-rally follow their competitors, clients, and suppliers. They will have the added advantage of understanding the industry and will be able to identify the subtleties that provide key clues. So if a salesperson sees that routine buying decisions are slowing down or that reorder quantities are smaller/larger, the guessing can become fairly accurate.

The power of the thousand-pound gorilla is mag-nified in the trade journals. Usually, there is a sub-stantial advertising budget that can be allocated as a reward. Reviews and exposé pieces can and are influ-enced. The piece may then be trumpeted outside the industry to the uninitiated. Most trade publications match content to sources of advertising to within a few percentage points.

Generally, the industry is aware of its own trends and there will be a series of articles over some time discussing the possibility of a breakthrough or improvement. This is euphemistically referred to as *speculation*. While the company may be guarding its intellectual property, the industry will engage in a lot of informed speculation and guessing. When this reaches into the mainstream financial press, momen-tum has already been building.

TAKE AWAY

COMPANIES INITIATE STORIES ACCORDING TO THEIR OWN TIMETABLES.
THESE STORIES WILL USUALLY HAVE A FAVORABLE SLANT WITHIN A
CRITICAL EVALUATION TEMPLATE.
MAINSTREAM MEDIA HAS DEADLINE PRESSURE, WHICH RESTRICTS
RESEARCH.
BE AWARE OF HOW STORIES JUMP FROM TRADE PUBLICATIONS TO
MAINSTREAM MEDIA.

Chapter 16
CEO Personality

When assessing an investment, company management is a key consideration. I challenge the reader to find one satisfactory investment that had poor management. Savvy IR practitioners realize the importance of the issue. When any senior executive or board appointments are announced, there is usually an impressive recital of accomplishments and expertise. Sometimes the announcements are borderline laughable, given the seriousness of their intonation.

What investors frequently forget is that while chief executive officers (CEOs) are obviously the key executives, there are management and executive teams behind them. Many CEOs are very well regarded within their industries. In some cases, they achieve their own brand status. Depending on the personality and the circumstances, the CEO will be positioned to have certain characteristics that investors will find attractive. The most obvious is the "turnaround specialist." They are usually perceived as hard-nosed and reality-based with ice water in their veins.

The more subtle version occurs when a company is attempting to create traction. CEOs will be branded to match the perceived company personality and potential investors. Characteristics such as frugal hard-working behavior will appeal to a certain market demographic (over fifty-five years of age rather than the young, hip, in-the-know crowd). This all helps the believability and likeability factor that helps sell the company. Whatever happened to "boardroom presence"? Now a CEO is assessed on media star qualities.

In some instances, the CEO personality achieves a cult status. The financial media seeks out comments and opinions from these individuals. When CEOs speak, markets not only listen—they also adjust valuations accordingly. Needless to say, those CEOs have done well in their media training classes.

When circumstances conspire to allow the CEO to become a Pied Piper, the market's objectivity diminishes. Most CEOs have suitable integrity for their positions. Make no mistakes and never go to sleep on this point: *CEOs have their own agenda.* They have normally been employed and incentivized to maximize stock valuation. They therefore speak from a position of "obligatory bias." They do not speak in the critically evaluative mode of an investor reaching a personal buy, hold, or sell evaluation.

This spotlight effect does not allow for the full range of opinions to reach the surface. Other CEOs have effective operations and find themselves overshadowed in the battle for mind space. Investors who are too easily influenced by dominating media presence will find themselves disappointed in a market correction when the dominance of ideas is re-aligned with realities. Usually, the experience is a very Darwinian process.

The CEO is influenced by what the market wants to hear. In rising markets, when all boats are rising, messages of prudence and caution are not overly welcome. As euphoria and expectations build, prudence is downgraded and sunny times ahead accentuated. This is why investors listen to the timbre of the voices as much as to the message when they listen to conference calls and webcasts. The market craves this serotonin fix. Like most addictive behaviors, you always need the next one to be a little stronger. And when the circle of co-dependence is disturbed or broken, the pain is described as a loss or breach of trust. Many CEOs cannot survive and the inevitable management change starts.

TAKE AWAY

NEVER ABDICATE COMPLETELY AND PLACE UNQUALIFIED TRUST IN ONE BUSINESS LEADER, ESPECIALLY IF THEY HAVE A LOT OF MOMENTUM.

Chapter 17
CEO Access

IR practitioners will be the first to admit that the chief investor-relations officer should be the CEO. The captain of the ship does have unique responsibilities and should be publicly accountable. This accountability creates a requirement for visibility. Given the time demands of operating most companies and dealing with the financial media and shareholders, there is a serious time conflict.

The CEO must first accept that they are the chief investor-relations officer. The IR functionaries, no matter how professional, competent, and diligent, are intermediaries of the staff officer variety. If the CEO wants the message to be heard, understood, and believed, they need to deliver it personally.

The IR staff can follow up, answer questions, amplify, color in details, bring up to speed, fill in background, build bridges, and establish media relationships, and so on. But we all know that the CEO is the commander-in-chief and the buck stops on the CEO's desk.

Some CEOs are more media and IR savvy than others. CEOs need to provide access. They must also see and be seen. If they drop off the radar screen, there is a danger that perceptions will run askew. If the CEO is not front and center, there may be storm clouds on the horizon. Please refer to the chapter "Cones of Silence."

TAKE AWAY

IS THE CEO FRONT AND CENTER?
IF NOT, WHAT IS THEIR COMMITMENT AND UNDERSTANDING?

Chapter 18
Chat Rooms

I have a major problem with the so-called tool known as chat rooms. While I believe in the freedom of expression, I also believe that anonymity allows individuals to shirk their responsibilities.

Most, if not all, chat rooms allow for individuals to register under a cloaked identity. The information provided to the chat-room operator is rarely and in some cases never verified. If you believe in the message of the chapter entitled "Whose Interests?" then why even go there?

Those who do not or cannot identify themselves post rumors, innuendo, naiveté, and, occasionally, a correct fact. Unfortunately, the chat rooms can and do influence the prices of some stocks. The more influence a chat room has on a stock valuation, the less attractive the stock is as an investment vehicle.

TAKE AWAY

FORGET ABOUT THEM!

Chapter 19
Cone of Silence

Companies don't always want attention. Sometimes they just want to be left alone. Much like checking on a young toddler who has become much too quiet, this is the exact time when we should be most attentive. Companies will attempt to bring down the cone of silence.

Some of the techniques will be obvious. Senior officers and regular spokespersons will not reach out and talk to their normal contacts, neither formally nor informally. Calls are not returned promptly. When the call is made, it's late and the chit-chat is positively dull. Writers, well aware that they must capture the minds of readers, despair. But should they?

Basically, a company wanting to impose the cone of silence will systematically break the rules of good communication and cause the media and investor community to go to sleep.

Executives will not attend conferences where they can engage in social chit-chat. If someone just has to do a presentation, you may find a junior executive suddenly has a moment of glory in the limelight. All the while, senior officers are hoping that the light-weight has minimal impact.

Taking a chapter from KGB standard procedures, management may create a diversion by allowing the

media and investors to focus on other issues. A
favorite trick is to issue a flurry of press releases
before the cone of silence comes down. The flurry will
hopefully absorb any current interest and cause the
marketplace to overload slightly and to conclude that
it's "too much, not going to listen for a while." As it
happens, the stealth bomber is being prepared for
flight, and management does not want you to observe
what is being loaded onto the bomb racks.

While not physically possible for the average
investor or most institutions, you almost want to stalk
key officers. Are they taking trips? Where are these
trips? Is there a pattern with these trips? Perhaps
they are visiting key clients or suppliers. There are
media tracking services that can place senior person-
alities at locations. Also, some of the fractional jet
rental and executive jet rental services can become
good sources of information.

If you suspect something is up, you have several
options. Call up the IR staff first and ask them directly. They will, of course, deny it or just make bland
statements about day-to-day activities. It's not the
response but the body language that will interest you.
When there is too much "nobody but just us chick-
ens," you know something is up.

At this point, the executive has not done anything
wrong. They are permitted to conduct company
affairs in privacy, even secrecy. You as an investor are
also permitted to anticipate corporate events and try
to get ahead of the curve.

One of the dangers is that senior officers are actually spotted with someone in a public place and the
rumors go ballistic thereby driving the stock. The
classic public response is to issue a press release indi-

cating that the company is working on a potentially significant event, which may impact share values. However, the conversations as yet have not been concluded and may not be concluded satisfactorily. If they are concluded, a press release will be issued at that time with full details. [Special note to senior officers: This is why we invented underground parking lots and private dining and meeting rooms, not to mention telephones and video conferencing.]

TAKE AWAY

STILL WATERS RUN DEEP.

Chapter 20
Quiet Period

The quiet period is supposedly, well, quiet. That's why it's called quiet. This is not a good time to have a nap. Sometimes it's referred to as a blackout period or a waiting period. The term has been knocked around so much that confusion reigns supreme.

The SEC at www.sec.gov/answers/quiet.htm attempts to address the issue. The first sentence states that the term is not defined under federal securities law. It then goes on to explain that the quiet period refers to the time frame from when a company registers a statement with the SEC staff to when the SEC declares the registration to be effective. The SEC continues with an explanation that there are some rules to be followed during this time. It also states that it encourages companies to continue making normal corporate announcements in the ordinary course of business. But don't forget: it's not a defined term.

Confusion manifests. The confusion of investors can be highlighted by a recent question dealt with at www.sec.broaddaylight.com/sec. The investor queries, "Before a company releases earnings, it seems there is a certain period of silence. How long is this 'quiet period'?" The answer refers you to the first SEC web reference and then goes on to explain, "There is no such thing as a 'quiet period' or period of silence before a company announces its quarterly or year-end results."

Confusion in the marketplace abounds. Most investors and the majority of IR staff do not understand the quiet period. How could they? The term is undefined, but it has rules. This is a classic regulatory conundrum, which easily breeds a sucker factor.

While the regulatory context is dysfunctional, there are still market forces attempting to "work it." The term "quiet period" is most frequently applied to the period that runs from the end of the quarter to when the earnings are announced. The theory supposes that management and insiders have access to information as it develops and therefore should not trade or make public comments until the final results are properly released. There is also a very real danger that before the entire reporting process is completed, information is fragmentary and incomplete.

As with any theory, there are pros and cons. The quiet period prevents senior officers and those in the loop from improperly taking advantage of insider information. They should refrain from making public comments prematurely and they therefore should not be in the media.

Given the law of unintended consequences, companies now have a diminished capacity to deal with rumors and innuendo. To the sharks looking to bounce the stock around, this is akin to blood in the water. Any piece of meat will do as long as it moves the price. The buzz is carefully selected given expectations in the marketplace. Shock value is nice because it is unexpected, allowing for trading traps to be sprung. (Bear traps and sucker rallies.) Officially, management must sit back, suck it up, and grit their teeth.

Given the preponderance of business-oriented media, many executive officers appear on public shows but do not discuss potential results that are imminent. They do, however, cover topics that have been previously disclosed, or which the SEC says are normal course announcements. Now you have senior officers communicating more mundane news. Why? It may hardly be news, but it can be reassuring and reaffirming. By having senior officers appear, you symbolically rally the troops to stand firm and dissuade negative rumors. They do not really say anything since they could seriously run afoul of the law. The media makes attempts to trap them but usually fails.

Media channels have First Amendment rights to free speech. By covering senior executives with star power, the media builds ratings. They are also playing the system and accentuating the anticipation factor. The media knows the senior officers must pick their spots and should not say anything about imminent earnings announcements. The senior officers know they are tiptoeing through a regulatory minefield. Savvy investors know they should listen to undertones and nuances. The exercise becomes eye candy, which at this point is not considered illegal or even inappropriate.

The illusion caused by the eye candy has a sucker factor. If results are taking a turn for the worse, the market will follow the Pied Piper right up to the abyss of bad news. If results are positive, then the investor will be late for the ride up. If the results are either as expected or inconclusive, then what the hell were you doing on TV and in the media? Promoting the stock, maybe?

One potential solution is to shorten the time frame of the "quiet period" and release earnings sooner.

This will compress the shark zone and restrict their power to maneuver (i.e. read or manipulate). More easily said than done since many companies are very large and require some time to complete the process.

A possible solution that has generated some discussion would be a continuous accounting process that closes and posts the results daily on the Internet. This would eliminate much of the volatility arising from surprises. You could actually monitor very small increments. Some businesses are reasonably well suited to this approach. As an example, a mortgage lender could accrue interest revenue and interest cost daily. Other normal operating costs such as salaries, rents, etc. could also be reserved daily.

Certain businesses that have choppier business models, causing swings from one week to the next, may prove to be more anxiety driven. Certain sales cycles are also monthly or quarterly driven so there are large bulges, which in the long run may not matter. The market may end up involuntarily micromanaging the company and suckering itself out of a good stock. Even the best running back fumbles the ball or loses yards on occasion. The competition will also be able to get a better handle on what is happening. Would you like a daily sales and profit graph of your major competitors?

The cost of converting to a very short-term accounting cycle is undetermined. Many small businesses would not be able to comply due to a lack of resources. Also, there would be a disintermediation effect given the normal trading hours of stock exchanges versus the location of head offices. When the NYSE and NASDAQ close at 4:00 p.m. ET, California is just strolling out to lunch. Monthly sounds like the best solution. Many companies already issue monthly sales figures (particularly, the automotive and retail sectors).

On Nov 3, 2004 the SEC has proposed rule 33-8501. This change would go a long way to rectifying the above criticisms. SEC staffers could not provide a timeline as to when the proposed rules would come into force, if they ever will. Investors continue to be vulnerable as information timing continues to be manipulated.

TAKE AWAY

BUY ON RUMOR, SELL ON NEWS IS AMPLIFIED DURING THE "QUIET PERIOD."

MARKETS ARE CONVERSATIONS AND SOMEONE WILL ALWAYS WANT TO TAKE CHARGE.

KNOW TO WHOM YOU ARE LISTENING.

KNOW WHEN YOU ARE LISTENING.

MANAGEMENT MUST STARE DOWN THE RUMOR SHARK DURING THE "QUIET PERIOD."

Chapter 21
Headlines & Embargoes

There are thousands of press releases issued daily. Large-scale public companies with sophisticated marketing-communications programs could issue several in one day. Not all would be considered material disclosure in the context of securities legislation.

During earnings season, you may have, at the peak, some five hundred to six hundred companies issuing results on the same day. The mechanics of issuing a press release have become very simple. So simple that those press releases are their own worst enemy. There are too many, making it hard to achieve mind space of any lasting value.

Writing press releases has become a skill and an art form unto itself. The headlines must captivate or die. Terms such as "record earnings," "record profits," and "record sales"—new this or new that—are all utilized to amplify the news. People usually remember the headline and forget the news. The more detail there is, the harder it is to communicate; the investor needs to be more attentive.

Press releases are issued through dissemination services such as Market Wire, Business Wire, or PR Newswire. The client pays a fee, usually not more than several hundred dollars per page. In exchange, the full text is delivered to numerous financial media sources, proprietary services such as Bloomberg, other news wires such as the Associated Press (AP), and a wide range of traditional print and electronic media sources. The two oldest firms charge by the word or page, making it uneconomic for smaller companies to communicate. The new guy on the block, Market Wire, charges a standard fee and does not restrict the size—this is true full text.

Moreover, specialty lists of key journalists, analysts, investors, and influencers are maintained. Once the press release has "crossed the wire" and has been disclosed, it will be e-mailed and/or faxed to these individuals. As the use of PDAs grows, the alert systems will deliver critical information right into your hand, your purse, and God knows where else.

Online and 24/7 news services such as Reuters, Bloomberg, CNBC, and others have news desks operated by editors who quickly scan incoming news. These editors will take the press release and expeditiously write a story about it. Very large companies are guaranteed to be picked up because of their size. Smaller companies can easily find themselves ignored.

Just do some quick arithmetic. Assume your news desk has four individuals. It's a high-pressure position with modest wages. If you have, for example, 1000 press releases coming through on any one shift, that equates to 250 cover-or-ignore decisions per person. Assume that they are committed to producing a lot of comment. Further assume that with 80% of the press releases, some kind of story is written and released. That becomes 200 stories per day, per person. You can push the math around but it's clear to understand this is not the way to earn a Pulitzer Prize.

The overwhelming conclusion is that the headline and the first paragraph are mission critical. If you have not made your case by then, forget it. The overworked staffer has moved on. If it does catch the eye, a story is written and put out. The story may look very similar to your press release. Entire phrases and sentences may have been borrowed. That's fine because now your story is being transmitted as reportage under a third-party byline with the sponsorship of a reputable news organization.

Due to time pressures, the potential sucker factor is at play as very little to no fact checking occurs. We have all heard of hoaxes (which are eventually discovered). What troubles me is the grey area when hyperbole turns into bent and then twisted fact. Too many people conclude that since a reputable news wire carried it, it must be true. The story does not have to be true; it just needs to get through.

Have you ever watched how volume can spike following an announcement in a press release? Naturally, everyone will tell you that there was news. Traders who are organically bonded to their computers and trading systems can react quickly and have the ability to make rapid-fire decisions.

You will see the price reacting to the news. Despite capital-market theory, it does take a period of time for the price to fully reflect the news. You frequently hear the terminology that the current price is fully valued or has discounted the news. No one has ever been able to calculate or measure this dynamic in terms of elapsed time.

Is there a seam that allows those in the know to take advantage? After all, it does take some time for the dissemination service to issue the press release and cross the wire. Various media outlets will rebroadcast or re-disseminate the information. The market then has to actually read the press release and come to a value judgment such as buy, sell, hold, or ignore.

Despite the lightspeed transmissions that occur, insiders can take advantage. Consider this scenario: a press release usually goes through several drafts. If there are two companies involved, there are two CEOs, two lawyers, two IR officers, etc. Both companies will want to issue simultaneously. Both companies may need to issue in more than one regulatory jurisdiction besides the U.S. The solution is to embargo the press release with the news wire and release at a pre-specified point in time (usually after board meetings have concluded or legal documents have been signed). The dissemination service will often record what may be referred to as a "time out." This is when the news was issued and crossed the wire. You have now achieved disclosure.

Some will argue that you need additional time for dissemination to occur. The press release needs to be read. Some companies actually request that their stocks are halt traded to allow for dissemination. But once that news has crossed the wire, it is very difficult, if not impossible, to argue that you have traded on insider information. So you trade to be ahead of the curve.

Some companies have ethical standards about when their employees and senior officers can trade. Standards and adherence vary. Ethics are not enforceable by securities law. Also, what constitutes an insider and who is in the loop is a problematic definition. Just look at the surges of volume before some announcements are made. In any event, every trade has some form of electronic time stamp. As long as your trade time stamp does not pre-date the "time out" that the dissemination service has recorded, many lawyers would conclude that you are clean; not fair, not ethical, but clean.

TAKE AWAY

**1000 PRESS RELEASES,
4 HEROIC AND OVERWORKED EDITORS,
250 COVER-OR-IGNORE DECISIONS,
80% THROUGHPUT CREATING 200 STORIES
PER EDITOR IN AN EIGHT-HOUR SHIFT,
25 STORIES PER EDITOR, PER HOUR,
EQUATES TO 2.4 MINUTES PER STORY.**

**WHAT CAN YOU INTELLIGENTLY WRITE IN
2 MINUTES AND 24 SECONDS?
HOW DO YOU MAKE A BUY/SELL DECISION?
SUCKER FACTOR POTENTIAL? RIGHT OFF THE CHART.
CAN SOMEONE GET IN AHEAD OF THE CURVE? CERTAINLY, THE
EMBARGO MEISTERS ABOUND.**

Chapter 22
IR DNA

What makes a good investor-relations officer? The media and analytical community have several opinions. Essentially, they want someone who knows what is going on; who responds quickly to only their phone calls and can give them as much poop as they want. There are people like that, and again, in the words of Billy Crystal, "You know who you are."

While IR officers have been known to hold the rank of senior vice-president at certain firms, they usually are vice-presidents or directors at most. The staff below them is typically senior managerial. There are few entry-level positions. At certain firms, the president conducts IR as an afterthought. Again, "You know who you are." Your investors probably also know.

A theoretical job description may contain some or all of the following parts:

The incumbent will report directly to either the president or the chief financial officer.

Develop and direct a comprehensive investor-relations strategy that incorporates direct contact with analysts, investors, and the financial media, creating realistic expectations of anticipated financial performance.

Internal relationships will include chairman, chief executive officer, president, chief operating officer, executive committee, senior financial management, corporate communications, corporate legal counsel, public-relations staff, and crisis committee.

External relationships will include securities regulators, legislators, external counsel, independent auditors, buy- and sell-side analysts, portfolio and money managers, stock brokers, investment bankers, individual investors, financial and industry trade press, opinion leaders, consultants, and vendors of investment-relations services.

Develop, maintain, and nurture constant and consistent communications with analysts, financial media, and investors through telephone, personal contacts, group meetings and written materials, conference calls, webcasts, and other Internet-enabled technologies.

Prepare, arrange, and participate with management for all presentations, questions, conferences, and one-on-one meetings within the financial community.

Understand and be well versed in the critical drivers involved in financial communications and models thereof.

Direct the design and production of signature-piece financial-communication collateral including (but not limited to) annual reports, quarterly reports, investor-relations portions of corporate web sites, and PowerPoint presentations.

Manage the annual shareholders meeting and quarterly conference calls and webcasts.

Develop investor-relations messaging and themes for the corporate-communications program.

Make presentations to analysts, investors, and financial media either one-on-one or in conference and meeting formats.

Establish and maintain an excellent understanding of the company's finances, operations, technologies, and core competencies.

Establish and maintain an excellent understanding of the industry's contextual realities and drivers.

Stay current on market opinions from investor and media sources regarding the company's competitive position and its comparison to competitors, potential competitors, and comparable companies enabling the incumbent to make strategic recommendations to senior executives.

Follow the company's stock price, volumes, accumulation/distribution, and other trading trends.

Review preliminary research reports submitted by the analysts for comments and provide prompt and accurate feedback to foster report accuracy.

Education: A college degree is required. Preference will be given to MBA, CFA, and/or degrees in communications.

Experience/Qualifications/Characteristics:

A clear and thorough comprehension of valuation models employed within the investment industry.

Understanding of the financial asset management industry with established contacts, excellent reputation, and credibility.

Strong interpersonal skills, superior intellect, ability to grasp complex issues, and an outstanding ability to communicate.

Energetic and resourceful team player.

Proactive worker with an attitude of continual learning.

Compensation: Commensurate with background and experience.

There is confusion about which talent pool should be tapped to provide personnel. Some have a print-journalism background and are wordsmiths. Some have an electronic-media background and understand the visual. Very few seem to have a good grasp of earnings before interest, taxes, depreciation, and amortization (EBITDA) or other financial concepts. Consequently, they are often treated with silent disdain by financial analysts and resented by journalists. A growing number of financial types are becoming noticeable. They understand EBITDA but seem to get ambushed by details they do not think are important. Typically, the last group emanates from the sales and marketing side of financial services. But no one seems to have a good grasp of the Internet.

TAKE AWAY

INVESTOR-RELATIONS OFFICERS FUNCTION AT THE HIGHEST STRATEGIC LEVELS.
INVESTOR-RELATIONS OFFICERS GUIDE ANALYSTS AND ACTUALLY REVIEW THEIR REPORTS. THIS HAS REGULATORY IMPLICATIONS.
ANALYST REPORTS DO NOT SHOW MANAGEMENT'S FINGERPRINTS.

Chapter 23
Corporate Communications

What are corporate communications? How are they different from marketing communications? How are they different from investor relations?

Corporate communications can best be described by showing examples. With the Enron debacle, a company called Dynergy ran a series of TV commercials informing people of what they do. The general public does not normally buy gas or coal in the quantities that Dynergy deals in. But a very substantial dollar was spent explaining what they do and how everyone benefits. Entities that need to buy energy valued in the millions if not billions of dollars are unlikely to be influenced by a thirty-second TV commercial (assuming the decision makers even see it). We can safely assume that the intent of the ad is not marketing communication.

There are many companies that engage in corporate communications. The way I understand the process, some of the intents are to raise the profile of the company with stakeholders who may be customers, clients, suppliers, partners, employees, action/pressure groups, unions, elected politicians, civil servants and regulators, or foreign governments. If you are an investor or a potential investor, you will of course be exposed to the effects of these ads.

I do not question the right or the legitimate need of publicly traded companies to advocate agendas and ensure that their interests are properly championed. There is a crossover point where corporate communications become a parallel investor-relations function. The crossover effect should be scrutinized within the sucker factor.

Corporate communications provide the publicly traded company with an alternative channel to reach investors. While financial communications and investor-relations communications are subject to a regulatory framework, corporate communications are not subject to anything more stringent than ensuring modest family-viewing ratings are not violated.

There is a behavioral and psychological aspect to investing. The *fear* and *greed* dynamic is rooted in emotion. Emotions may run hot. Emotions may run cold. Emotions are subject to influence at all times. Investing is based upon confidence. Nominally, confidence builds its cornerstone or foundation on financial statements. Over time, the investment mosaic has allowed for perception of the company to be integrated into the thought process. This allows corporate communications to ride into the landscape and influence an investment decision.

Most corporate communications will attempt to accentuate, enhance, and develop the themes that the company is smart, clever, strong, unique, special, trustworthy, at one with the Matrix, responsible, sensitive, etc. Whenever the positive perception of the corporation can be enhanced, you are strengthening the investment proposition that the company offers. The opposite is also true.

TAKE AWAY

CORPORATE COMMUNICATIONS PROVIDE THE SUBLIMINAL CHANNEL INTO THE INVESTMENT MOSAIC.

Chapter 24
Investment Conferences

Investment conferences are a pre-Internet, pre–Reg FD dinosaur designed to make someone, usually an investment dealer, look good. Typically, a conference would be held at a posh resort that is well known for an agreeable climate. Such conferences are hosted by investment dealers whose objective is to help attendees gain investor insights. Attendees would typically be analysts and portfolio managers who would place buy and sell orders through the investment dealer. Publicly traded companies would present at these conferences.

The investment dealer would play two sides of the fence. The brokerage side wanted to curry the favor of institutional investors who would generate enormous commission revenues. The investment-banking side wanted to curry the favor of companies who would pay enormous underwriting fees when they issued capital. To make the conference work, the publicly traded companies needed to provide compelling insights into their affairs so that institutional investors would have a good reason to attend.

All parties sought advantage over others within the market. Public companies competed for attention and favor. Investors competed for information, which would improve their value judgments. Dealers and brokers competed for transactional revenues.

The entire raison d'etre was, and remains to be, information. No one at this level is really pathetic enough to travel thousands of miles just for the buffet. With the advent of Reg FD, companies insisted that their remarks be webcast and available on the Internet so as to ensure full, adequate, and immediate disclosure. Needless to say, the savory tidbits were no longer offered in the same manner.

Given the select nature of the audience and the Reg FD effect, these conferences are no longer as important as they used to be. But they do retain a schizophrenic and retro character. Some corporate executives complain of having to go to too many. ("I am so popular; I have to manage my time and exposure." It's nice to be important, isn't it?) Certainly, investment conferences are not the appropriate platform to release new information, but you do want to retain your A-List status as a guru or speaker. These conferences were effective at allowing a lot of private and informal one-on-one meetings in a social environment. This allowed companies to promote themselves and ensure the corporate message was getting through.

TAKE AWAY

LARGE DEALERS, LARGE COMPANIES, AND LARGE INSTITUTIONS HAVE ALWAYS AND WILL ALWAYS PLAY A LARGE GAME. ORDINARY MILLIONAIRES AND SMALL INVESTORS ARE NOT INVITED.

Chapter 25
Arms Merchants

When you observe most IR departments, even at the largest of companies, there is only a handful of employees pushing the buttons and pulling the levers. How do they do it?

To the knowledgeable practitioner, there is a very wide array of professional service providers who are the arms merchants of the IR business. No publicly traded company could exist without them. Rarely do these companies have a public persona. These anonymous or low-profile entities provide much of the infrastructure that is relied on by both the sinners and saints.

Full-text news wires have one of the longest tenures. These services have their roots in the days of telegraph and then Teletype services that would transmit your telegram over their own proprietary networks. The IR officer will use them to deliver a press release to multiple points such as financial news media, Bloomberg, other quote vendors, etc.

The term *full text* is critical. The regulator requires that a company's press release be issued from source and delivered to the disclosure points without anyone changing a word. Usually, the regulators and stock exchanges will review the dissemination circuits or channels and determine that they meet minimum disclosure standards. The media and other services can then opine, comment, rewrite, self-confuse, and pontificate at will.

The company is only legally liable for what they have issued. The media and others, however, may misunderstand the message. The corporation's regulatory responsibility stops at the full-text press release. Media outlets have the First Amendment protecting them even if they have made a mistake. (Usually the problem is blamed on the company with an accusation of miscommunication. I am not aware of anyone in the media admitting that they did not listen properly and missed the point.) I have always found it interesting that many IR officers review analyst reports but not media stories, yet both entities are considered independent. Should we try to level the playing field?

The wire services are built on legacy systems, which have been added to over time. There are numerous modems and connections to a wide variety of third-party systems. You may occasionally experience a delivery failure, which is not always the wire service's fault. But as the wire service sends you the inevitable bill, they get blamed. Sometimes the wire-service staff are centered out and verbally abused by vengeful IR staff who are not doing their job very well but need a scapegoat.

Wire services are starting to offer smart press releases that integrate multimedia features. Companies may now send PowerPoint slide shows, pictures, spread sheets, PDFs, Flash content, and more. Most companies stick to the full text at the present, but as broadband grows on a retail level, the stakes will go up.

Web-site templates are designed for the predictable

IR activities. Services that provide standard templates are a godsend since most internal IT functions are not up to the dynamic challenges of making changes and additions on a moment's notice.

The template can be frosted up to accommodate individual corporate looks and branding standards. Since they are all subject to the same regulatory regime, they should all be doing the same things in the same manner. What really happens is that no one provides substantive insight. It's all bland vanilla pudding in a variety of interesting containers.

The IR officer, who has proactive discretion on what goes up and when, manages the template. Some IR officers readily admit that they get very busy and neglect to update. As long as someone does not shout at them, they get away with it.

Webcast services take advantage of a new technology that came out of the Internet and experienced an adoption rate in the IR world that was unprecedented. With the advent of streaming media and Reg FD, most, if not all, self-respecting companies now webcast a quarterly conference call.

IR webcasts typically require you to download a player from either Microsoft or Real. Apple has something called QuickTime, which has a small share in the IR world. Real has recently started charging for their basic product and Microsoft offers theirs with their basic system. The webcaster pays license royalties depending on which system and volumes are used.

There are the actual webcast service providers that are really plugged into what are called continuous delivery networks (CDN), which help to move the webcast efficiently. Part of the broadband phenomena, they will webcast anything from a jazz festival to internal corporate communications. There are also aggregation services that offer efficient access to webcasts for publicly traded companies. Most were once free. The survivors are, not surprisingly, moving toward a fee model.

Annual report design & production used to be the signature piece for most companies. The design industry successfully raised the ante over the past decade and many companies have been issuing glossy and expensive works of art that explain the companies' values, brand image, and so on. Ultimately, glossy works are not helpful to the investor.

There is a backlash as both investors and companies do not want to be caught in the sucker factor. Many companies are experimenting with a black and white, plain paper, no pictures approach. The costs are cheaper and the electronic versions are lighter and easier to deliver.

Some companies are experimenting with a living annual report. The living refers to the dynamic aspect, which is really a Flash movie that may be upgraded and changed. These are expensive to produce and somewhat gimmicky. In reality, if revenues have dropped 10% for whatever reason, they have dropped 10%. Color paper, brown paper bags, or Flash movies will not change it.

The financial statements are frequently accompanied by a variety of charts. A picture is worth a thousand words. But the sucker factor comes into play when you look at the scope of graphical design play. Charts are designed to promote the company story, so beware. Also, they may not necessarily be consistent from year to year. Graphics can be influential in many different ways. You have to be careful in determining how the message is massaged.

TAKE AWAY

THE ULTIMATE RESPONSIBILITY FOR THE MESSAGE LIES WITH THE COMPANY.
THE ULTIMATE AND SOLE RESPONSIBILITY FOR COMPREHENDING THE MESSAGE LIES WITH THE INVESTOR.
THE DEVIL HAS MANY TOOLS.

Chapter 26
Institutional Clout

No one will argue that the institutional investor is, and will most likely remain, the dominant financial player for the foreseeable future. Many IR programs may even dedicate a specific individual to curry favor with this thousand-pound gorilla. Companies will frequently go on the road and meet with key institutional investors, analysts, and portfolio managers just to keep everything warm and fuzzy.

Institutions are beholden to their performance ratings. In a hyper-competitive environment, funds are measured on monthly, quarterly, annual, and long-term returns. They also know that they are essentially looking at the same universe of stocks. The difference comes down to who can move ahead of the curve, either in or out.

The sucker dynamic can be quite perverse. The company is selling its story. This creates push energy and the company is looking for validation and support. The portfolio manager has the high cards and is in a position to extricate unique or advantageous viewpoints. Companies in pre–Reg FD used to do this all the time and everyone understood the game.

Institutions are at the top of the food chain. Broker positions have been diminished, so now the top dog has less natural flow. Institutions can lean on a company, stay in the regulatory shadows, and seek a better view of the company. The carrot is continued support or increased support for the stock. The stick is the move to sell. Ladies and gentlemen, this, of course, is poker. How good are your cards? How good are your nerves? Because, good people, there are no ladies and no gentlemen playing in this game. It's just the good and the dead.

Certain institutional investors have reputations for expertise in certain stocks and are seen to be leaders. Institutional holdings are reported in numerous public fashions. If the major knowledge player is selling, what conclusions are you supposed to come to?

Institutions that also buy debt and/or convertibles hold a potential trump card. The analytical framework is different. When you give security, you have to answer questions. You also give collateral and report on many features more than once per quarter. The angle is just very different and more comprehensive. There are contractual reporting responsibilities.

The pure equity investor, even the large one, does not have this information flow. Institutions manage their exposure to any one name. There are risk committees, which expand or contract the limits. Depending on the funds you are managing, if you are happy with the stock, you should also be prepared to buy the debt. The debt should have less risk and moves you up the information food chain. The chief investment officer is going to listen to all inputs and steer the mother ship accordingly.

It's always hard to discern, but when the prettiest girl at the ball stops dancing the fast rumbas and wants to sit down . . . well, you figure it out.

TAKE AWAY

MIGHT MAKES RIGHT!

Chapter 27
Disclosure

Disclosure is like a bikini: what it reveals is exciting; what it conceals is critical. Financial communications and investor relations are disclosure-driven functions (the revealing part). The concept of disclosure is driven by what is considered material. For smaller companies, life is edgier. Almost anything can therefore be material. For larger companies, a lot can be hidden by relative scale (obviously the concealment, or, if you prefer, the critical part). Bombshell announcements are, of course, press released, conference called, and webcast. Most of this news is at the top of the mind channel where a company has no choice.

Disclosure is also managed so that select items on which the company may not want to focus, but must release, are disclosed in a non-prime-time fashion. Say what? There are ways of doing things in a discreet fashion to avoid ruffling the feathers.

Management frequently does have visibility. It is particularly aware of what may be viewed negatively. They perhaps have been questioned in the past or the media has caught something and has written it up. Areas such as environmental concerns, executive stock options, super voting rights for key controlling shareholders, or contracts between parties that may have a potential conflict of interest are just a few that are vulnerable.

Basically, management will do a slow dance and start releasing bits and pieces of information. These bits and pieces may not seem interesting at the moment, as other factors have more presence and visibility. The transaction is managed so that a major announcement is not necessary, allowing for the information to be bled out a drop at a time.

In the end, management has not only disclosed, but has repeatedly disclosed, warned, or attempted to communicate on the point. Being accused of poor communication is not a criminal or civil infraction. Many executives, if discovered, apologize publicly and contritely that perhaps they have not communicated the point very well. Management does not go to regulatory jail, but the shareholder has been punished.

The SEC requires a huge number of documents to be registered routinely. Another batch of documents is required for special announcements and amendments. Most filing requirements are time driven. That is to say, they follow the quarterly reporting cycles. Consequently, a lot of companies file several documents all within the same relatively short time frame. Not unlike the riverboat gambler who can elegantly riffle the deck and make it look like a fair game.

Most investors are not even aware of all the requirements. Corporate web sites link to EDGAR and the SEC, but who really reads all this stuff? 10-Ks and 10-Qs, etc. are all written in a compliance-correct, but sucker-factor manner. Management has the ability to hide in plain sight. Huge documents are filed. Information overload is played upon. And it's all there for anyone who wants to read it and think about it. It's all there on page 74, paragraph 16.2, section IV, subsection ii, that may be appendixed to exhibit 3.

TAKE AWAY

IF THERE WERE SERVICES THAT WOULD PROMISE TO SOBERLY READ SEC FILINGS AND POINT OUT THE SMALL NUGGETS, I WOULD SERIOUSLY CONSIDER USING THEM.

Chapter 28
Safe Harbor

The best has been saved for last. Corporate executives have a unique advantage: they can and often do engage in financial promiscuity. Being clever and averse to risk, they also use protection at the same time. The prophylactic of choice is the "safe harbor clause."

The safe harbor clause is the rather perverse child of the Private Securities Litigation Reform Act of 1995. Apparently, too many companies were being sued and/or were afraid of being sued by investors who had listened to an executive officer sound positive. The investor relies on the officer's comments and invests. Consequently, if there is a lawsuit, it's because the investor has some kind of grievance relating to losses of their wealth.

Corporate executives felt vulnerable and achieved protection through legislation. While I am not a fan of the frivolous and nuisance lawsuit, the safe harbor clause provides an inordinate amount of protection for the corporate executive, allowing a sucker factor to develop. The safe harbor clause provides so much protection and legal impedimenta that certain corporate executives have realized that they can get out there and make the extreme price-juicing visionary statement with very little concern for any negative consequences.

Evidently, the prophylactic value of the legislation has become a one-way affair. The investor does not have any comparable protection. The corporation, which is in a satiated state of protection, moves on while the investor is constantly cautioned about the risks of investing and therefore remains in a state of anxiety.

This balance is not adequate or satisfactory. The only tangible recourse is for the investor to spurn the company. Even large sophisticated investors are rarely inclined to litigate. This is not conducive to encouraging capital formation.

For the interests of the reader, I have included a safe harbor clause that frequently appears on materials, including documents filed with the SEC:

This report contains certain "forward-looking statements." The company desires to take advantage of the "safe harbor" provisions of the Private Securities Litigation Reform Act 1995 and is including this statement for the express purpose of availing itself of the protection of such a safe harbor with respect to all such forward-looking statements. These forward-looking statements, which are included in Management's Discussion and Analysis, describe future plans or strategies and include the Company's expectations of future financial results. The words "believe," "expect," "anticipate," "estimate," "project," and similar expressions identify forward-looking. The Company's ability to predict results or the effect of future plans or strategies is inherently uncertain. Factors, which could affect results, include [company would include most of the relative operating issues that they normally encounter in running their business]. The factors should be considered in evaluating the forward-looking statements, and undue reliance should not be placed on such statements.

Some companies have the gall to further state:

We refer you to our form 10-Ks, 10-Qs, and 8-Ks that we have filed with the SEC. They may discuss new or different factors that may cause actual results to differ materially from those forecast. For further information, please view XYZ Company's most recent SEC filings.

TAKE AWAY

HOW DO YOU INVEST MONEY AND NOT PUT UNDUE RELIANCE ON WHAT COMES OUT OF THE MOUTHS OF TOP EXECUTIVE OFFICERS?

The Devil Made Me Do It!

I have received e-mails with various versions of the following. Clearly, this is something to think about:

A person dies and is negotiating her final destination with Saint Peter at the Pearly Gates. Saint Peter says, "Normally we are clear on relocation, but in your case, we are going to give you an opportunity to choose. You will have the experience of both worlds so that you can make your decision."

Her first stop was a day in hell where she found herself enjoying a country club setting with friends and relatives who were having a super fun time. Next, she spent a day in heaven where she lived in peace and serenity while floating on a cloud.

Afterwards, she said to Saint Peter, "I never thought I would be saying this, but hell is more my style." With that decision, she was promptly escorted down to hell where she was met by the Devil, who awaited her with the satisfied grin of a winner.

Looking beyond him, she saw a bleak dismal place with nothing but suffering. Alarmed, she cried, "What's happening? I was here yesterday and this was a living paradise!"

The Devil responded, "Yesterday you were being recruited. Today you get to experience the real thing."

TAKE AWAY

IT'S TIME TO THINK FOR YOURSELF.

Financial Sucker Test

Character is fate. Are you a sucker? What about family members, friends, or that person at work? Take the test and see. Send this test to someone else and see how they feel about it. An online discussion is available at www.bloglines.com/blog/financialskeptic.

How do you find investment opportunities?

- Broker recommendations
- Business media
- Comments from friends and associates
- Subscribe to newsletters or analytic service
- Shrewd observation of the business and investment scene
- Chat rooms and e-mail alerts

How much time per week do you spend on your investments?

- Under one hour
- One to two hours
- Two to five hours
- Five hours or more

How many advisors have you consulted in the past five years? (Spent about a half-hour hearing them out.)

- One
- Two
- Three or more

Have you ever lost money on your investments? (Paper loss or cash.)

- Yes
- No

Why did you lose the money?

- Defrauded
- Stock just suddenly dropped
- General market conditions (everything went down)
- Unanticipated bad news
- Bad advice from broker/advisor
- Really do not know (be honest, be *very* honest)
- Company declared bankruptcy

If a stock drops more than 8 to 10% what do you do?

- Sell position
- Sell position and wait to re-enter at a lower price
- Do nothing
- Buy more and average down

Why do you buy a stock?

- Liked the story
- Noticed trading volume or price change
- Recommended by advisor
- Recommended by friend/family member
- Recommended by a newsletter or analytic service

When you buy a stock, do you have a target price in mind?

- Yes
- No

Why do you sell a stock?

- Bad news
- Changing technical picture
- Recommendation of advisor
- Recommendation of friend/family member
- Recommendation of a newsletter or analytic service
- Found something better

How do you monitor an investment?

- Read press releases, quarterlies, and annual reports
- Listen to webcasts/conference calls
- I wait for someone to say something. (Honestly!)
- Follow the business media

Financial Sucker Test
Interpretation

The reality is that the financial world and life in general must operate on trust. Any society that does not trust will not thrive. For proof, just observe the results of any repressive regime on any level.

However, because we choose to trust, it is possible to be abused. Therefore, on any given day, anyone can be taken advantage of. These abuses are usually small or inconsequential. Unfortunately, sometimes they are not.

As hard as it may be, when our trust is broken, we must not become so jaded that we are unable to trust again. In doing so, we end up punishing ourselves much more than any penalty that may be awarded a wrongdoer. Rather than depend on the faulty shield of a lack of trust, we can develop our perceptions and help catch the greedmongers who want to take advantage of our better side. Here are some thoughts:

How do you find investment opportunities?

It all has to start somewhere. If you are just walking down the path of life and are prepared to easily accept someone else's ideas, you lose responsibility for yourself and control over your circumstances. A casual well-intended comment from an acquaintance is usually not framed in your context. The business media is necessary for a general overview of business conditions. The media will only deal effectively with the larger companies. Chat rooms are a great source of toxic and dubious information. Brokers, newsletters, and analytical services typically have integrity and track records that can be assessed. They do not provide guarantees and need to be critically evaluated.

Many will tell you that you attract what you project. My suggestion is to work on what your investment objectives really are and then to focus your search in that context. There are approximately twenty-five thousand companies that trade on various stock exchanges across North America. You simply have to formulate a strategy that at the outset is emotionally and psychologically appropriate to you and then stay in that framework. This will help you determine if a company's story or investment proposition resonates with you.

How much time do you spend?

Investing is not a hobby that can be set aside when you do not feel like it. In a certain sense, investing may be more important than your day job. If you delegate the function, time should be minimal. If you want to manage your investments directly, then your time expenditure will be easily over five hours per week. Otherwise, you will not be aware of the most obvious facts and certainly will be suckered.

How many advisors have you consulted?

Advisors are more appropriate for the novice or relatively new investor. Someone needs to teach you a few things. You learn by asking those that know. Brokers/advisors know more than you do. Different brokers and advisors will have different perspectives on the same issues. Need I say more?

Have you lost any money on your investments?

Investing is a full-contact sport. You will not learn much, if anything, until you lose some money. Ask yourself what you learned and do not forget it. By the way, the really good investors also learn from mistakes made by others. It's much cheaper.

Why did you lose money?

This is perhaps the hardest question. Also, good answers will give you the most profitable results. We learn from our mistakes. You have to be honest with yourself and know what they are.

If a stock drops . . . what do you do?

The market is always right. Do not argue with the tape. If market participants decide to get out, there must be a good reason. If you stand in the way of a stampeding herd, you will be trampled. A dropping stock price means the company is not worth as much. Investors need to have "life-boat drills."

Why do you buy a stock?

You need a defensible reason. If you do not have a well-formulated reason, you do not have context and therefore will not be able to adequately manage your position in the future. In short, if the information for the reason is changing, you need to reassess your viewpoint.

When you buy . . . do you have a target price in mind?

Knowing when to sell a stock is perhaps the hardest investment decision. There is lots of advice on when and how to buy. Very little advice exists on when and how to sell. This in part accounts for the negative emotionalism usually associated with a sell off. The major dynamic that dominates at this point is one of fear and confusion, closely followed by panic. This is not the preferred context for making a decision. To avoid the poor emotional and psychological environment, an investor is well advised to set a target price. This should provide direction and guideposts to follow. Ideally, a sell should be viewed as a victory as you have successfully reached your objective and are now realizing your profits.

Why do you sell stocks?

Other than reaching the target price, what will motivate you to sell a stock? This really is the mirror image of "why did you buy the stock?" Again, if you operate in a vacuum, you will be suckered and not realize it. Your brokerage statement, however, will provide you with an accurate accounting of your losses.

How do you monitor your holdings?

This is perhaps the most important question faced by investors. Once you have a position, there are three ongoing decisions: continue to buy, start selling, or maintain your hold. You are making this decision continuously in real-time every second that the market is open. Many investors are in default mode and are not conscious that they are in fact making decisions. How many times have investors lamented, "Oh, I wish I had sold"? While there are many ways to monitor an investment, the most important issue is to actually monitor and assess your investments. Annual reviews are too far apart. [Hint: Many daily financial papers have weekly reviews on weekends when you have more time.]

Affirmation of Renewal

This is to certify that I _____
have achieved sucker status.

On more than one occasion, sometimes as a serial offender, I have tried many foolish moves mostly without success.

Such dubious stratagems as hunches, hot tips, Internet rumors, office gossip, throwing darts at the financial page, and listening to family members (who are not rich anyway) have been extensively explored.

Quasi-defensible techniques such as penny stocks, chat rooms, momentum investing, suspicious e-mails, strange newsletters, and intermittent reliance on the general news media, as well as some stuff I never really understood but that sounded good have proven to be less than reliable.

I have lost money, been disappointed, experienced frustration, and sometimes have questioned the capitalist free-market system.

However, *I seek redemption, renewal, and investment profits. I move to understanding, internalizing, and truly appreciating the concept of caveat emptor: Buyer beware.*

Therefore, I will become responsible to myself. For if I am not responsible to myself, how can I hold others to be responsible to me?

TAKE AWAY

BE GENTLE WITH YOURSELF.

Glossary of Selected Financial Terminology

Action The price movement and volume of a stock or overall market.

Affiliated person A person who is able to exert influence on a publicly traded company, usually resulting from a minority share position.

Autex An electronic system that notifies brokers when another broker wants to buy or sell a large block (which is then traded as usual, on an exchange or over the counter).

Back testing The process of optimizing a trading strategy using historical data and then seeing whether it has predictive validity with current data.

Beating the gun Getting an advantageous price in a trade through the quick response to market activity.

Blow out The quick sale of all shares of a new stock offering.

Bubble theory The belief that stock prices rise substantially above their intrinsic or fundamental value until, at the same time, the bubble bursts and prices plunge.

Bulk segregation Client-owned stock held in street name but kept separate from brokerage-owned securities.

Capping Placing selling pressure on a stock in an attempt to keep a low price or to force the price lower. Violates various exchange-trading rules.

Closing tick The number of stocks that ended trading on an uptick minus the number of stocks that ended on a downtick.

Congestion A term relating to the technical analysis that observes a series of trading sessions in which little or no price movement occurs.

Deal stock The stock of a company that is rumored to be a takeover target.

Digested securities Stocks purchased by investors who will probably hold them for long periods of time.

Dirty stock A stock that does not meet the requirements for good delivery.

EDGAR (Electronic Data Gathering Analysis and Retrieval) SEC's system used by public companies to transmit required filings.

Miss the price Having an order in hand but failing to execute a transaction on terms favorable to the client and thus be negligent as a broker.

MOMO play Investments acquired only on the basis of momentum without any concern for fundamentals.

Painting the tape An illegal practice where securities are bought and sold creating an illusion of large volumes and significant interest. This may draw unsuspecting investors to buy, enabling the painter to profit.

Securities analyst No one is sure any more. In days of old, there was a noble guild, which was virtuous and honorable. Their word, reputation, and integrity were everything. They suffered defeats caused by treacherous behaviors and were subsequently scattered to the far and distant corners of the markets. Some true believers dream of their return. Some of the very weak brethren dream of getting a better day job.

Sleeper Stock with a small following that has the potential for big moves when the story gets out.

Spoofing Manipulation tactic where traders with a position in a stock will place anonymous buy orders in large volumes and then cancel the orders. The stock price jumps and draws in others from the unsuspecting and naïve. Many view this as one of the causes of increased volatility.

Ten bagger A stock that has gone up ten times in value.

Vetoing stock A class of stock that allows the owner to veto critical corporate matters. It usually does not include the right to elect board members.

Wallflower Sometimes called an orphan, it is a stock that has been ignored by analysts because it is too small or it's in an out-of-favor sector. A prime target for value investors.

About the Author

George Gutowski considers himself to be a former arms merchant within the investor-relations industry. After completing a masters of business administration (MBA) from Concordia University, he has worked with several large North American financial institutions.

His unique background led him through various positions of increasing responsibility with investing and lending authority within the capital markets.

During this time, he began to observe how individuals and companies acted when they needed and wanted money. The lessons and conclusions learned (usually the hard way) were many. The major lesson was that even the best financial statements did not always explain everything. There usually was a story to go with the numbers. The more reliance placed on the story, the less useful were the statements. But every story had best be listened to. It was then a good idea to look directly into the eyes of the recipient and "do a basic gut check."

In the recent past, he has held marketing responsibilities with a traditional full-text news-wire service and most recently with webcasting services specializing in financial communication.

In these positions, he had the opportunity to closely observe the investor-relations business. There he met a few outrageous sinners and more than one sanctimoniously pious, but ethically challenged, company. He still needed the gut checks.

Observing that the investment business is very high profile, but that the investor-relations business is more arcane, he decided to write this book based on his personal experiences and observations of various investor-relations programs for large-, mid-, small-, and micro-cap companies.

This is his first non-fiction work. He unfortunately has come to realize that some of the internal institutional reports he wrote on why certain investments and/or loans were good risks turned out to be fiction. We are all on a journey. Thank God he was able to use other people's money.

He may be reached via e-mail at georgegutowski ebox@hotmail.com. He will attempt to respond to e-mails in a timely fashion. This book marks his crossing from arms merchant to warrior-author.